Micah
Better than rivers of oil

by Gerald Gerbrandt

Faith and Life
Bible Studies

Faith and Life Press
Newton, Kansas

Will the Lord be pleased with thousands of rams,
  with ten thousand rivers of oil?
Shall I offer my firstborn for my transgression,
  the fruit of my body for the sin of my soul?
He has showed you, O man, what is good.
  And what does the Lord require of you?
To act justly and to love mercy
  and to walk humbly with your God

(Micah 6:7-8, New International Version).

Copyright © 1985 by Faith and Life Press, Newton, Kansas 67114
Printed in the United States of America
Library of Congress Number 85-81305
International Standard Book Number 0-87303-105-9
The publishers gratefully acknowledge the support and encouragement of the
Congregational Resources Board of the Conference of Mennonites in Canada in
the development of this book.

Design by John Hiebert
Printing by Mennonite Press, Inc.

Better than rivers of oil

Table of contents

Introduction

Micah plunges us headlong into the world of the Old Testament. He's one of the prophets, those fearless messengers who spoke forthrightly for God and who turned the tide of Hebrew history.

In Micah, we see how prophets did their work. They looked at the events of their day from God's point of view. They felt the concern of God for the welfare of the nations and right dealing in the marketplace. God moved in their lives and in the lives of those who heard them.

The prophetic understanding turns up almost everywhere in the Old Testament and flows into the New Testament.

So, we must meet Micah. This study will take you through the book which carries his oracles. An oracle is the poetic form in which a prophetic saying was captured, remembered, and carried from one person to another, from one generation to the following generation. Eventually, the oracle was written on paper and so it came to be passed on to us. Perhaps not all prophetic speech was in symbols intertwined with dramatic lines, but most of the sayings that were remembered carry the striking form of oracles.

The eight sessions in this book will guide you step by step through Micah. In order to gain most from this study, follow the steps suggested below.

First, work through the study guide by yourself. Read through the assigned Bible passage several times, watching for special details, as well as for key words and ideas. In getting acquainted with the passage, consider these questions:

* Why did the author write these words?
* What did the writer want to share?
* Why is this message important?
* What meaning do these words have for us today?

If you are working through this book with a group, write down your own answers to the questions before meeting with others. The more each person prepares ahead of time, the more fruitful your discussion will be.

Encourage everyone in the group to take part. Be flexible and feel free to use this guide in whatever way benefits you and your group most.

The Bible text used in preparing this study has been the New International Version (NIV).

Session 1. God sent a timely messenger

Micah 1:1

This first verse introduces us to the Book of Micah. In this session, we want to use it as a window into Micah's world.

In order to better understand the message of Micah, we need to know something about the world and times in which the prophet lived, and to which he spoke. What was the mood of this world? What forces moved the thoughts and actions of people in those days?

We will also try to learn what we can about Micah. Although this opening verse does not call him a prophet, it clearly means to show him as one. We'll learn more about the meaning of being a prophet as we go along.

And, finally, we will survey the book which grew out of Micah's preaching. These are the words of the Bible through which God can and does speak to us. As we begin this study, let us open ourselves to these words.

Small town's view of some mighty armies

"The word of the LORD given to Micah of Moresheth during the reigns of Jotham, Ahaz and Hezekiah, kings of Judah—the vision he saw concerning Samaria and Jerusalem" (1:1).

1. Most prophetic books of the Bible begin with a brief note about the prophet. Compare this one with those in Isaiah 1:1, Hosea 1:1, and Amos 1:1.

Where was Micah's home?_____

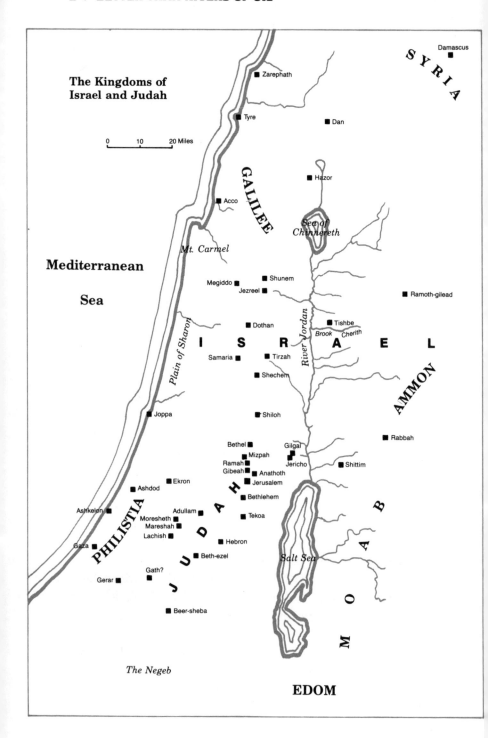

The Kingdoms of Israel and Judah

0   10   20 Miles

SYRIA

Damascus

Zarephath

Tyre

Dan

GALILEE

Hazor

Acco

Sea of Chinnereth

Mt. Carmel

Mediterranean

Sea

Megiddo

Shunem

Jezreel

Ramoth-gilead

Dothan

Tishbe

Plain of Sharon

Brook Cherith

River Jordan

I S R A E L

Samaria

Tirzah

Shechem

AMMON

Joppa

Shiloh

Rabbah

Bethel

Gilgal

Mizpah

Jericho

Ramah

Shittim

Gibeah

Anathoth

Ekron

Jerusalem

Ashdod

Bethlehem

Ashkelon

Adullam

J U D A H

Tekoa

Moresheth

Mareshah

Lachish

Hebron

M O A B

Gaza

Beth-ezel

Salt Sea

PHILISTIA

Gath?

Gerar

Beer-sheba

The Negeb

EDOM

Find on the map the place where he lived.

When did Micah preach?_____

What are we told about Isaiah and Hosea but not about Micah?

_____

What other things can you observe from these verses?

_____

_____

Notice how little information we really do have about Micah the prophet. If we are to learn more about him, we will need to find it in his preaching itself.

Moresheth was a small village about twenty-five miles southwest of Jerusalem. Its special location gave it more power than its size would otherwise suggest. It stood at the edge of the foothills overlooking the coastal plains.

Armies marching toward Jerusalem would come through these plains and had to pass by Moresheth. As a result, the kings of Judah had built a number of forts within a few miles of Moresheth. Military officials and officers from Jerusalem would have been a common part of the life of this rural community. Micah's preaching, no doubt, would have been influenced by the things that he saw these royal officers do.

Hezekiah as Assyria's bird in a cage

2. *Jotham* (742-735), *Ahaz* (735-715), and *Hezekiah* (715-687) were kings of Judah during the painful last half of the eighth century B.C. This was the period of Assyria's return as the military power of that part of the world.

Both Israel (the Northern Kingdom) and Judah (the Southern Kingdom) had just gone through a period of prosperity but both were now on the decline. In fact, in 722 B.C., Assyria put an end to the Northern Kingdom when it captured Samaria, its capital. Judah, during the reign of Ahaz, came under the control of Assyria. In 701 B.C., Assyria attacked many of the towns of Judah. Its army also camped outside the walls of Jerusalem but did not enter or destroy the city.

According to the Bible, King Ahaz led Judah away from faith in God (2 Kings 16:1-4, 10-16) whereas King Hezekiah is described as trying to take Judah back to faithfulness (2 Kings 18:1-6).

What are two things that King Ahaz did to earn this bad reputation?

a) _____

_____

b) _____

_____

What did King Hezekiah do to deserve a good evaluation?

_____

_____

The Bible gives us a brief report of the events of 701 B.C. (2 Kings 18:13-16). According to the diary of Sennacherib, king of Assyria, he captured forty-six Judean cities, and confined Hezekiah in Jerusalem "as a bird within a cage." Describe the mood such events would have caused in Judah.

_____

_____

This was the time of Micah: a day when faith in God was low, but a period when efforts were being made to restore that lost faith; a time of strength and weakness. Most of Micah's preaching came during this important time of testing toward the end of the eighth century B.C. The people still remembered the glory of their past days of prosperity. Some still assumed that nothing had changed. But Judah's power and wealth was quickly slipping away and religious faith was in danger of being lost.

Although King Hezekiah worked toward reform, his royal court and his officers had received their training under King Ahaz and may not have supported the new direction.

Prophets with the word of the Lord

3. Micah's preaching is described in verse 1 as the "word of the LORD." This phrase is often used in the Bible for the message of the prophets. See Hosea 1:1, Joel 1:1, and Zephaniah 1:1 for other examples.

When the preaching of the prophets is called the "word of the LORD," what does that imply?

_____

_____

How do you think the prophets received their message from God?

_____

_____

It is not uncommon to call the sermon in our worship services the "word of God." What does this suggest to you? How do you feel about this?

_____

_____

_____

4. Micah was a prophet. What would be your definition of a prophet?

_____

_____

_____

_____

A prophet has sometimes been defined as a messenger a) with the word of God, b) to the people of God, c) in a time of crisis, d) with the goal of increasing faith and obedience. Compare this with your own definition.

Do you think the world still has prophets today?

_____

Who would you consider to be modern-day prophets?

_____

_____

_____

Compare these persons with the four marks given in the definition above. Do they fit?

_____

Oracles of judgment and salvation

5. Read through the Book of Micah. Although this will not be easy reading, it should only take ten to fifteen minutes. When you have read a paragraph give it a title, and describe its mood. Use the terms optimistic or pessimistic for the mood. Prophetic messages (usually called oracles) are often divided into words of judgment or doom and words of salvation. Use the following paragraph divisions for recording your titles and descriptions of mood.

1:2-7 _____ (title)

_____ (mood)

1:8-16 _____ (title)

_____ (mood)

2:1-5 _____ (title)

_____ (mood)

2:6-11 _____ (title)

_____ (mood)

2:12-13 _____ (title)

_____ (mood)

3:1-12 _____ (title)

_____ (mood)

4:1-5 _____ (title)

_____ (mood)

4:6-13 _____ (title)

_____ (mood)

5:1-5a _____ (title)

_____ (mood)

5:5b-15 _____ (title)

_____ (mood)

6:1-8 _____ (title)

_____ (mood)

6:9-16 _____ (title)

_____ (mood)

7:1-7 _____ (title)

_____ (mood)

7:8-20 _____ (title)

_____ (mood)

Notice that the Book of Micah, like most other prophetic writings, does not tell a story that runs through the book. Rather, it is a series of loosely connected prophetic oracles (parts of the prophet's sermon). These oracles are usually in poetic form. And because the connection between the oracles is not always clear, this makes prophetic books hard to read through. We are used to reading material organized around a logical pattern.

In these days of our danger

The prophets of the Old Testament were not scattered evenly thoughout the years of Israel's history. Rather, they tended to be bunched around the times when the people of God were in trouble. In times of danger and testing, God sent messengers to Israel. These prophets made plain to the people what God required of them: faithfulness and obedience.

Most will agree that we are living in a time of turmoil and danger unlike that faced by any other people in the world's history. That the world might be destroyed in a nuclear war is a real possibility. The faith of the church is also under attack—directly, and perhaps even more dangerously, indirectly by the values and assumptions of our society. It is essential for the church to retain its witness in this time. This is just the type of situation to which God sent prophets in Old Testament times.

I believe this raises two questions every Christian needs to face. 1) Am I listening for and heeding the words of God's messengers to today's church? 2) Am I being called to be one of God's messengers to that part of the church round about me? Consider these questions carefully and prayerfully.

Session 2. Howl like a jackal and moan like an owl

Micah 1:2-16

We now come to the Book of Micah itself. Given the nature of the material, we will need to move slowly and orderly. Don't feel bad if, on your first reading, many passages seem unclear. This will change.

Chapter 1 introduces the book as a whole. Verses 2-5 reflect the book's basic announcement—God is coming in judgment. Verses 6-7, then, apply this to Samaria in the Northern Kingdom and verses 8-16 apply this to Judah. The rest of the book will then go into more detail.

The fact that chapter 1 serves as an introduction to Micah shows that this book is following a plan and is more than just a record of the prophet's preaching.

Although we cannot tell exactly how long Micah served as a prophet, signs are that he was active for a number of years. Surely, he preached more than a total of ten minutes (the time it would take to deliver the parts of his sermons contained in the book). So, only a limited number of Micah's oracles are recorded. At some point after the time of Micah, some editor produced the book using Micah's oracles. But only a few were used, and these were arranged according to subject, and not in the order that they were spoken. In this way, Micah 1 then introduces the book.

God treads on the high places: 1:2-5
1. These four verses move clearly and orderly from one

point to the next. The thought of each verse, or part of a verse, builds on the one that went before it. Read these verses carefully, and outline this flow of thought in your own words.

1:2a _____

_____

1:2b-3 _____

_____

1:4 _____

_____

1:5 _____

_____

2. The first two lines of this section call on all peoples of the earth to pay attention. God is going to announce something important. Normally, prophets addressed Israel, the Old Testament people of God (remember the definition of a prophet given in the last session). But here Micah expands the audience to take in everyone in the world. Why do you suppose he did this?

_____

_____

_____

3. Write down the three phrases used to describe God's action in verses 2b-3.

a) _____

b) _____

c) _____

Prophetic oracles are a form of Hebrew poetry. A key feature of Hebrew poetry is parallelism—a way of saying the same thing in parallel ways. So, the three different ways in which God's action is described here should not be seen as three different types of activity, but as different ways of saying the same thing: *God is coming!*

Which phrase of the three do you think might be the most helpful in understanding God's action at this point?

---

4. Verse 4 announces the effects of God's coming. Compare this verse with Judges 5:4-5 and Isaiah 64:1-3. All of these passages speak of God coming to act in the affairs of people. What do these phrases have in common in the way they speak of God?

What do you think it means to speak about God in this way?

Scholars use the word *theophany* to describe those events in which the glory of God's presence is shown to humans. One of the best examples of this in the Old Testament is God's coming to Mount Sinai to give Israel the law (Exod. 19). Judges 5:4-5, Isaiah 64:1-3, and Micah 1:2-5 are further examples. When God comes, all of nature is affected. The God of the Bible is the God who created everything, and who can call on the powers of the universe to support God's will.

As a rule, however, when God is spoken of in this way, God is seen as coming to defend Israel from its enemies. Israel then looks forward to God's coming since that means deliverance. But now Micah stands this common way of speaking on its head—God is coming to act, he says, but this time, God will attack the very people chosen by God.

5. The reason for God's coming in judgment is now given. It will be helpful to look at the meaning of a few of the words in this verse.

Transgression/sin. These are two words for wrongdoing. Transgression suggests a conscious rebellion against God and what God requires. Sin has more the meaning of missing the mark, whether done on purpose or not. The two terms are used side by side in this verse, both drawing attention to Israel's guilt. The meaning is that God's coming in judgment is justified.

Jacob. Jacob was the father of the twelve tribes of Israel. In the first part of verse 5, this term applies to all of Israel, in keeping with this common way of speaking. In the second part of the verse, it is used to contrast the kingdom of Israel to the nation of Judah. The use of Samaria, the capital city of Israel, shows that it refers only to the Northern Kingdom.

Israel. Israel is often a problem word in the Old Testament. It can mean one of three things: a) It can be a general reference to the Old Testament people of God. It is then a religious term. This is the way Israel will be used in these lessons on Micah. b) It can refer to the nation when it consisted of all twelve tribes, during the time of Saul, David, and Solomon. This is usually known as the United Kingdom. c) It is the name of the Northern Kingdom with the ten tribes which broke off from the South after the time of Solomon.

In this verse, it is used in the religious sense, and like the first reference to Jacob, with which it is parallel, it refers to the people of God.

Samaria. Samaria was the capital of Israel, the Northern Kingdom. It was thus the political and religious center of the Northern Kingdom. Here was where the nation's leaders lived and worked.

Judah. Judah was the name of the Southern Kingdom. Its capital was Jerusalem.

High place(s). Worshipers of the Canaanite gods commonly built their altars on hills, or on any piece of higher ground. This phrase, thus, became a code word in the Old Testament, a symbol of Israel turning from God and going after the gods of the Canaanites. In this verse, the phrase draws attention to the fact that this forsaking of God has even reached the capital city, Jerusalem.

Samaria made a heap of rubble: 1:6-7

1. Verses 2-5 introduced this chapter, and the book as a whole. Now we come to the first firm announcement of punishment. The focus is on the Northern Kingdom and its capital, Samaria. This city is mentioned in the introduction to the book (1:1), and in verse 5, but this is the only specific oracle against it in the whole book.

List the phrases used for the destruction of Samaria.

_____

_____

_____

_____

2. What hints do these verses give as to the reason for this punishment?

_____

_____

_____

3. The references to prostitution may be misleading. Canaanite religion was a nature religion. Being most concerned about the cycle of seasons, the Canaanites practiced certain fertility rites as ways to assure the growth of their livestock and their crops. Thus, they sought to control the rhythm of nature.

Annually, the death and resurrection of their god Baal would be reenacted. The rituals associated with such worship included sexual intercourse with religious prostitutes. Using the logic of sympathetic magic, these worshipers hoped that such actions would encourage the gods to imitate their acts and bestow fertility to the soil and herds so much needed in an agricultural society.

Israel, as it took over many of the farming practices of the Canaanites, often also accepted some of these fertility rituals. So, the references to prostitution in verse 7 are not an accusation of simple sexual immorality, but rather an indictment of the Northern Kingdom for adopting this part of the religion of the Canaanites.

4. Both the Old Testament and Assyrian records note that Assyria captured Samaria in 722 B.C. This oracle probably refers to this event. Read 2 Kings 17 for an account of this defeat, and an interpretation of it. What reasons does that chapter give for the the fall of Israel?

Incurable wound at the city gate: 1:8-16

1. The focus now shifts to Judah, and the villages surrounding Micah's hometown. Counting Jerusalem, twelve geographical sites are mentioned. Try to find as many as possible on the map in Session 1. Unfortunately it is not known where all of the cities listed are located. It is probable, however, that they were within a few miles of each other, and close to Moresheth, the city where Micah lived.

2. List all the references to suffering, or mourning, or statements which would have negative meanings for the people living in the area.

---   ---

_____   _____

_____   _____

_____   _____

_____   _____

The mood of the passage is clearly set by these references. An Israelite would also have noticed that the whole passage has the form of a funeral dirge. All cultures have customs for mourning the death of a person. This passage reflects the kind of lament which would have been spoken in Israel. Here Micah takes such a form and pronounces it over Judah. Death may not yet have arrived, but it is coming.

3. The English translation cannot catch the word plays present in the original Hebrew. Somehow the name of each city becomes the basis for a statement about it. It is as if someone today would say "The place called Victoria will henceforth be called the Place of Defeat," or "Tacoma will give off a terrible aroma," or "The City of Brotherly Love will become The City of Hateful Shove." Hans Walter Wolff has translated this passage in a way which attempts to retain some of this technique.

> 10 Don't "boast" in Gath! Weep; yes, weep!
>   In Dustville roll yourselves in the dust!
> 11 You inhabitants of Horntown,
>   they are blowing an alarm for you on the ram's horn.
>   Rootberg will be uprooted.
>   Lament for Standton,
>   your standing place shall be taken from you!
> 12 How can the inhabitants of Evilland hope for good?
>   Indeed misfortune is coming down from the Lord
>   upon the very gates of the City of Fortune (Jerusalem)
> 13 Harness the steeds to the chariot,
>   ye inhabitants of Chariotsburg (Lachish)!
>   (That is the chief and first sin of Zion's daughter,
>   for in you are found Israel's rebelliousnesses.)

14 Give parting gifts to Gath's Possession (Moresheth-Gath)!
   Deceitville's fortifications
      are a deception for Israel's kings.
15 I am bringing an army of occupation upon you,
      you inhabitants of Occupation town (Mareshah).
   The glory of Israel is coming to hide
      in the Refugee's Hiding Place (Adullam).
16 No hair on your head as you howl in mourning
      for the children you loved!
   Bare yourself like the beaked bird (the eagle),
      in mourning for your children who are leaving you
      and going into exile.[1]

4. Notice verse 13. The only reference to the nature of Judah's sin is found in this verse. Lachish was the largest and most important city of the region, and so it had become the major defense fortress. The charge, "this was the beginning of sin," may be related to this special place that Lachish had in the life of Judah.

Could this verse be suggesting that Israel's sin lay in its trust in military defense?

_____

_____

Where should Israel have put its faith?

_____

_____

What might this say to us in our time?

_____

_____

[1]Hans Walter Wolff, *Micah the Prophet.* Copyright © 1978 by Chr. Kaiser, Verlag, Munich, Federal Republic of Germany. English translation copyright © 1981 by Fortress Press. Used by permission of Fortress Press.

5. In 701 B.C., Assyria's armies once again marched into the land of God's people. According to Assyrian records, forty-six of the cities of Judah were taken, and Jerusalem itself was surrounded. Those events explain these verses. Just as Assyria earlier destroyed Samaria, Micah now announces, Judah will also experience the evil of Assyria's power. The effect will be felt in all the cities of the area, right up to "the very gate of my people,/ even to Jerusalem itself" (v. 9).

6. Now compare 1:2-5 with Revelation 2:12-17, one of the letters to the seven churches. Although the style is very different, both passages speak about God coming in judgment to a people which has committed itself to God, but which is not being faithful. Write Revelation 2:16 here.

_____

_____

What do you think "the sword of my mouth" might mean?

_____

_____

_____

Now think about your own congregation. What would you consider to be its major transgressions? List at least three.

a) _____

_____

b) _____

_____

c) _____

_____

What can and should you do about these?

_____

_____

_____

_____

7. Does a ceremony of mourning for a congregation's lack of faithfulness have a place in our churches today? What form might it take?

_____

_____

_____

What would be its purpose?

_____

_____

_____

Make God's coming a welcome event

Throughout all ages, God's people have called on God to come and help. The psalms, for example, are full of such requests. And this is the way it should be. God has demonstrated through actions in history that God is a redeeming and saving God. God loves us, and wants to help us when we are in need.

In light of this, I find Micah's message, especially in 1:2-5, unsettling. Here he uses Israel's traditions which spoke of God coming to deliver the people for a very different purpose. Yes, God comes to deliver, but God can also come to judge and punish. It is interesting that, in the Old Testament, the prophets' message tended to be one of salvation when circumstances were bad, and one of judgment when Israel was prosperous, and believed it was experiencing the blessings of God. Where are we at today?

Is God acting to deliver the people of God, or is God coming to punish us?

Or, more personally, can I comfortably pray the common table grace which begins with "Come dear Lord, and be our guest . . . "? Do I really recognize that my invitation to God to come may be an invitation to God to judge me?

My prayer is that my life will be such that I can welcome God's coming.

Session 3.Disaster planned for those who defile

Micah 2:1-13

Prophets were preachers, not writers. Their messages were delivered live to the people, probably in settings not ideal for preaching. Today preaching is usually limited to the formal church service. One person is given the floor and twenty-five minutes. As the sermon is presented, the congregation will normally sit quietly in the pews and either listen or daydream. Interruptions are rare.

Old Testament prophets did not have such an ideal place, or such agreeable listeners. Israelite worship tended to focus on drama, sacrifice, and ritual rather than preaching. Prophets had to create their own settings and audiences. This meant they spoke on the street, in the markets, at the gates of the city, or in the court of the temple. Wherever people tended to gather, there the prophets would go to deliver their message.

Although Micah 2:1-13 is in the words of Micah, it reflects a setting that provided an opportunity for debate and challenge. Not all of Micah's listeners were happy with his words and so they argued with him. Micah responded. In fact, his message built on their reactions. This back and forth exchange can still be detected in this passage.

Talking back to the prophets: 2:1-13

1. In order to understand this chapter, we must be aware of who is speaking at each point, and on whose behalf the

person is speaking. Sometimes Micah speaks for himself, sometimes he speaks with the words of God, and sometimes he quotes the words of those who oppose him. At one point, Micah speaks on behalf of God who is described as quoting the words of the people.

Read through the chapter, listening for the sounds of different voices. Decide whose words Micah is using at each point. Record your answers below for each verse. When you are finished, check your answers with the key at the end of this lesson. You may find it a little easier if you use the Revised Standard Version (RSV) for verse 6:

> "Do not preach"—thus they preach—
> "one should not preach of such things;
> disgrace will not overtake us."

2:1-2 _____

2:3-4 _____

2:4b _____

2:6-7a _____

2:7b-11 _____

2:12-13 _____

Coveting fields and houses leads to woe: 2:1-5
1. We noted in chapter 1 that Micah used the style of a funeral lament in his announcement of what will happen to Judah (vv. 8-16). Funeral customs continue to supply Micah with images in this passage. Cries of *woe* were a familiar feature of laments over the dead. In the customary lament, the opening "woe" would be followed by the name of the person who had died. The prophets used this form of speech to tell their listeners that they were acting in a way which would eventually lead to the grave. In prophetic speech, the "woe" would be followed by the specific actions which were being attacked.

Isaiah, a prophet in Judah around the same time as Micah, used this form six times in Isaiah 5:8-23. List the actions Isaiah denounced.

a) _____

_____

b) _____

_____

c) _____

_____

d) _____

_____

e) _____

_____

f) _____

_____

2. What are the two terms used for wrongdoing in verse 1?

_____   _____

In 1:5, Micah used the words *transgression* and *sins*. Life in Judah during those days gave Micah a rich list of words for sin.

3. The key word in this section is *plan* (v. 1), or *planning* (v. 3). What plans is Micah attacking in verses 1-2?

_____

_____

_____

_____

To which one of the actions attacked by Isaiah can these plans be compared?

_____

_____

4. What are God's counterplans—the plans God is making to defeat the plans being made by the people?

_____

_____

_____

5. What does the first line of verse 2 suggest is the root or basic cause of the people's plans?

_____

Compare this with Exodus 20:17. List the items referred to in this verse.

_____	_____
_____	_____
_____	_____
_____	_____

Notice how the last phrase covers everything, making it clear that the first part of the verse only gives examples.

Notice also how this final commandment is a climax to the Ten Commandments, and indirectly speaks to a number of the others, especially those dealing with relations between people. The most common reason for murder (#6) is the desire for personal gain, an example of covetousness. Adultery (#7) begins with an improper desire. Stealing (#8) begins with the yearning for someone else's property. The setting for the commandment on bearing false witness (#9) is probably a court case with a neighbor. It is not hard to see that such a suit may have risen from a dispute over property.

The meaning for the other commandments of this commandment suggests that it is not accidental that it is the final one. It sums up the commandments that went before it.

6. Whose plans do these verses suggest will be the more powerful?

_____

7. The meaning of verse 5 may not be entirely clear. When Israel originally received the Promised Land, it was divided among them by lot (Josh. 14:1-5). This was done at an assembly of the people. Micah is announcing that "in that day" (v. 4), when the punishment comes, those people who cheated others of their land will not have anyone to represent them. Thus, they will not receive any land when the land is again redistributed. So, the crime and the punishment are related—the landholders will become landless.

8. The judgment of verses 1-5 is of people who plot evil, and who have the power to carry it out. Power is one of the gods of all times. Most of society, including most of the church, strives after power. Although each of us may differ greatly in the amount of power each of us has, compared to most people in the world, all North Americans have a lot of power. And that includes you and me.

Examine your own life. Suggest some ways in which you use the power you have for unjust ends.

_____

_____

_____

Pascal, a French philosopher in the seventeenth century, said, "Justice without power is powerless. Power without justice is tyrannical. Justice and power must therefore be connected so that what is just is also powerful and what is powerful is also just" (_Pensees_, 298).

9. What a person covets often shows where a person's values lie. It reflects a person's ambitions and hopes. What does your coveting say about you?

_____

_____

_____

_____

An enemy hankers for windbag prophets: 2:6-11

1. The translation from the RSV suggested earlier for verse 6 is a much more literal rendering than that given by the NIV. The verse is not referring to prophets but to the fact that the people are responding to Micah's preaching with the retort "Do not preach to us about those things."

The Hebrew text simply reads, " 'Do not preach,' they preach, 'Do not preach concerning these.' "

Their challenge to him to stop preaching is a form of preaching. As the last line of the verse shows, the people feel sure that they are safe, and that God will not punish them. They consider Micah out of line for speaking about such things.

According to this verse, the people tell Micah that the things he is preaching about should not be preached about. After all, Micah is preaching about the use of money and power, and about social issues. Such charges are often made about the church today. The church, some people say, should limit itself to religion, and not become involved in issues that are the concern of the state. But can one really make such a distinction?

Can you think of any issues today which you would consider improper for a sermon topic today? If so, what might some be?

_____

_____

Suggest some social issues (or political or economic) about which you believe the church should be preaching.

_____

_____

_____

2. Verses 6-7a make it clear that some among Micah's listeners objected to his message. Who do you think such people might have been?

_____

_____

Micah responds (v. 7b), however, that some will find his message to be good. Who are they?

_____

3. List the crimes mentioned in verses 8-9.

_____

_____

_____

What do these acts have in common with what the prophet reported in 2:1-2?

_____

_____

4. A prophet addressing self-secure people who are oppressing the poor can speak with emotion and sarcasm. Verse 11 is an example. To say that what the people would really appreciate is a windbag (the real meaning of the word behind the NIV *liar*) who tells lies and predicts a future of "wine and beer" is strong language. But

prophets were not shy or wishy-washy. Micah had seen and perhaps experienced the impact and power of investors who kept on buying more land and causing poor people to become even poorer. Not only did these people abuse their power, they also felt that God was on their side and would protect them. Arguing with such an audience was sure to bring out strong language.

5. The major issue in verses 1-11 is injustice. Compare these words with those of Amos, another Old Testament prophet of almost the same time, as found in Amos 2:6-7; 4:1-2; 5:12. What are some examples of injustice in our world today?

_____

_____

In your country?

_____

_____

In the community in which you live?

_____

_____

Delivered by a shepherd king: 2:12-13
1. Dramatically, the mood changes. Until now Micah had accused the people of sin and announced punishment. Now, he holds out hope.

What image is used for God in verse 12? (Hint: it is the same as that of Psalm 23.)

_____

Read Psalm 23 and list four or five statements made about God's protecting power.

_____

_____

_____

___.

_____

2. Write down the phrase that is used twice of God in verse 13, and which is reinforced by the final line of the verse.

_____

What image is used of God in verse 13 (second last line)?

_____

What characteristics of God are suggested by this image?

_____

_____

_____

_____

3. Do you think the words of hope in verses 12-13 are addressed to the same people as the words of judgment in verses 1-11?

_____

If not, to whom do you think the hope was given?

_____

If yes, how would you relate these two quite different emphases?

_____

_____

_____

_____

Control the dreams that lead to acts
The first verse of this chapter suggests that frequently acts of injustice have their origin in the dreams of some-

one in bed. Sleepless hours in the night or the period between going to bed and falling asleep are often a time of fantasies and dreams. This is a time when secret thoughts can overtake us and we can give free rein to our imagination. This is often where scheming and sly plans begin. Micah recognizes the potential of this time period.

Micah addresses people who have the power to carry out those plots. But the clear warning given by the prophet also needs to be heard by those of us who may not have this same kind of power. Jesus warned his listeners that both hate and murder were sin. It has sometimes been suggested that dreams should not include actions which would be wrong if acted out. This takes self-control and practice. Prayer at bedtime is a form of protection from such temptation. May God control both our thoughts and our actions.

KEY for exercise on Micah 2:1-13, page 21.
>   2:1-2: Micah for himself
>   2:3-4: Micah is announcing the words of God
>   2:4b: God is announcing what the people will say
>   2:6-7a: the opponents of Micah
>   2:7b-11: Micah for himself
>   2:12-13: Again, the words of God

Session 4. Darkness of the hidden face on temple hill

Micah 3:1-12

Micah was a prophet from farm country. This chapter, however, makes it clear that he also delivered his message in Jerusalem, at the center of power in his nation. Here the king lived, and here his officials and his government's administrators had their headquarters.

Micah, the prophet from the rural countryside, went to the city and spoke his scolding words right in front of those who opposed him. Imagine how these city folk looked down on Micah. Consider the courage it took for Micah to act as he did.

One voice in three oracles: 3:1-12

Micah 3 contains three distinct although clearly related oracles. Each one is addressed to the leaders of the land. One can easily imagine the scene as Micah confronts this powerful body with his unwelcome message. The response of his hearers isn't given here, but it probably wasn't favorable.

The oracles themselves have a fairly consistent structure, with each containing an address, an accusation, and an announcement of punishment.

Micah 3:1-4

1 Then I said,
"Listen, you lead-
ers of Jacob,
you rulers of the
house of Israel.
Should you not
know justice,
2 you who hate
good and love
evil;
who tear the skin
from my people
and the flesh from
their bones;
3 who eat my peo-
ple's flesh,
strip off their skin
and break their
bones in pieces;
who chop them up
like meat for the
pan,
like flesh for the
pot?"
4 Then they will
cry out to the
LORD,
but he will not an-
swer them.
At that time he will
hide his face from
them
because of the evil
they have done.

Micah 3:5-8

5 This is what the
LORD says:
"As for the proph-
ets
who lead my people
astray,
if one feeds them,
they proclaim
'peace';
if he does not,
they prepare to
wage war against
him.
6 Therefore night
will come over
you, without vi-
sions,
and darkness, with-
out divination.
The sun will set for
the prophets,
and the day will go
dark for them.
7 The seers will be
ashamed
and the diviners
disgraced.
They will all cover
their faces
because there is no
answer from
God."
8 But as for me, I
am filled with
power, with the
spirit of the LORD,
and with justice
and might,
to declare to Jacob
his transgression,
to Israel his sin.

Micah 3:9-12

9 Hear this, you
leaders of the
house of Jacob,
you rulers of the
house of Israel,
who despise justice
and distort all that
is right;
10 who build Zion
with bloodshed,
and Jerusalem
with wickedness,
11 Her leaders
judge for a bribe,
her priests teach
for a price,
and her prophets
tell fortunes for
money.
Yet they lean upon
the LORD and say,
"Is not the LORD
among us?
No disaster will
come upon us."
12 Therefore be-
cause of you, Zion
will be plowed
like a field,
Jerusalem will be-
come a heap of
rubble,
the temple hill a
mound overgrown
with thickets.

Leaders and prophets in the royal court

1. The three prophetic oracles of Micah 3 have been
printed side by side to make it easier to see their parallel

nature. It should also help in the following exercises.

First, to whom is Micah addressing these words? Record this for each oracle.

Oracle #1 _____ (v.1a)

_____ (v.1a)

Oracle #2 _____ (v.5a)

_____ (v.7a)

_____ (v.7a)

Oracle #3 _____ (v.9a)

_____ (v.9a)

_____ (v.11a)

_____ (v.11a)

_____ (v.11a)

The last line of verse 1 shows that the leaders whom Micah is addressing were persons who should be concerned with justice. This is confirmed by the final two statements in verse 9. Although the terms *leaders* and *rulers* of verses 1 and 9 may suggest general names for leaders, it is possible that these were special titles for those who were responsible for the legal system.

Deuteronomy 1:9-18 describes the origin of this legal system. Notice Deuteronomy 1:13-15 where Moses appoints such officials. The next two verses (16-17), then, describe the task of these officials, and how they were to fulfill it. How were they to judge?

_____

_____

_____

_____

Most of the prophets whose words are recorded in the Old Testament had no part of the official leadership of the nation. Rather, they seem to have been outsiders to the power systems of their day. They were common people whom God called to deliver a message. Amos, for example, was a shepherd from the small town of Tekoa.

The Old Testament makes it clear, however, that in addition to the prophets who had a message from God there were many other prophets in Israel who were employees of the royal court. First Kings 22 tells the story of the true prophet Micaiah (often called Micaiah ben Imlah so as not to confuse him with Micah) and his challenge to the 400 official prophets active in the court of King Ahab. These 400 were the kind of prophets spoken to in verses 5-9.

2. Each oracle includes a specific accusation against the group confronted. Write down the crime of each group in your own words.

Oracle #1 _____

_____

_____

_____

_____ (vv. 2-3)

Oracle #2 _____

_____

_____

_____

_____ (v. 5b)

Oracle #3 _____

_____

_____

_____

_____

_____ (vv. 9b-11)

The crime in the first oracle sounds much like the op-
pression of the poor mentioned in Micah 1 and 2, and so
we will not discuss it further here.

Peace proclaimed when the people pay
The crimes of the second and third oracles are new, although hints about them appeared earlier. (See 2:11.)
Both stress that the message or verdict of the leaders
(prophets, priests, judges) is determined not by a word
from God, or truth, or justice, but by the hope for financial
reward. Verse 11 makes this quite clear.

An important duty for priests in Israelite society was to
teach the law and recall the story of God's actions in
Israel's history. This, no longer, was being done properly.

Judges were to follow the guidelines laid down in
Deuteronomy 1:16-17 (and also Deut. 16:18-20 where
bribes are clearly mentioned), as we saw earlier. They
were not to put a price on their verdicts. But self-interest
had now become the crucial concern. Imagine how it must
feel when people cannot trust the judges and the courts to
deal fairly with their problems.

Prophets from God should deliver God's word regardless
of the consequences. But here it says that these prophets
proclaim "peace" when a reward is promised to them, and
"war" (probably, curse) when no gift is offered.

Here the word _peace_ means more than the absence of
fighting or hostility. It implies total well-being, including
health and good feeling among the people. It is a way of
pronouncing a blessing upon those who hear the
prophet's words.

Deuteronomy 18:18 makes it clear from where a prophet
should get his message. Write this verse here.

_____

_____

_____

_____

What are some examples today where prophets proclaim peace when this is not part of the picture?

_____

_____

What standards can the church use to help it tell the difference between those whose message comes from God, and those whose message has been shaped to please the audience?

_____

_____

Most churches in North America today have a system of paid leadership. Do you think this makes it likely that these leaders may be influenced in their speaking by their salaries?

_____

What could be done to protect the freedom of such leadership, or to help them to be faithful to God?

_____

_____

_____

_____

Ruin and rubble in Zion

3. The accusation in the oracles against the leaders is followed by the announcement of punishment. Record this for each oracle.

Oracle #1 _____

_____

_____ (v. 4)

Oracle #2 _____

_____

_____

_____ (vv. 6-7)

Oracle #3 _____

_____

_____ (v. 12)

The emphasis in the first two oracles is on the fact that God will not be available to the leaders. The language used here reminds us of some of the psalms of lamentation. The leaders are not basing their judgments/words upon God, and thus God will be hidden from them.

Verse 12 is the climax of the first three chapters. Jerusalem is the city chosen by God. Its leaders and its people believe that it will always be protected by God. But Micah says the city will be completely destroyed. The name used here for Jerusalem is *Zion*, a name that stresses the fact that God has chosen it. All the theology of Israel's leaders would have to be reexamined if Jerusalem were destroyed. And yet Micah announces that this will happen.

What do you think would have been the people's immediate reaction to such an announcement?

_____

_____

_____

About 600 years later, Jesus spoke about Jerusalem and the temple in much the same way. Read Luke 19:41-44. Do you think Micah might have felt like Jesus did when Micah made his statement?

_____

_____

Read how the statement of Micah in 3:12 is referred to in Jeremiah 26:1-19. What, according to these verses, was the response of Judah to Micah's words?

_____

_____

What was the reaction of God to their response?

_____

Does Jeremiah 26:18-19 suggest that Micah's prophecy was not fulfilled? How can one explain this apparent difficulty?

_____

_____

_____

For Old Testament Judah, Jerusalem symbolized its special tie to God. It has been suggested that today the institution of the church is that sign of God's presence in the world. Could God ever make such a statement about the church? Is it possible that the church could forsake God to the point where God would say to the church, "You will become a heap of rubble"?

_____

_____

4. Verse 8 stands out in this chapter because there Micah shares how he understands himself. He starkly sets himself over against the false prophets of Jerusalem. Micah is not moved by profit (in fact, his words may endanger his life), but by the gifts of God. List what this verse

says Micah is filled with.

_____ __   _____

_____   _____

The last word of the four would possibly be better translated by the term *courage.*

Where, in the church, do we see such traits, or qualities?

_____

_____

How do you think you could receive such qualities and confidence?

_____

_____ __

_____

Dreadful the silence of God

I am especially struck by the punishment proclaimed in the first and second oracles (vv. 4, 6-7). In our age, it is hard to see the silence of God as a punishment equal to the destruction of Jerusalem. But that is the way it appears in this chapter.

I want to share two thoughts on this. First of all, the punishments announced in the Book of Micah tend to be tied to the particular crime. Prophets and judges who do not base their words on God will experience silence from God. But this truth can also be applied to everyday life.

When one pays attention and listens for the word of God in Bible study, devotions, meditation, discussion, and prayer, then God becomes available to us. Then God speaks. Too often we do not pay enough attention to this part of life. We can easily become so busy that we forget to speak and listen to God. I am also guilty of this. Our punishment may then be that God will hide from us. The danger in this area is, of course, that we may be so busy that we will not even notice the punishment. In other words, we will not miss God and thus will not be warned that we are in real danger. Let us be aware of this.

Secondly, it needs to be stressed that this is real punishment. This becomes clear when one reads some of the psalms of lament.

The Bible has few lines more powerful and tormented than "My God, my God, why have you forsaken me? / Why are you so far from saving me, / so far from the words of my groaning? / O my God, I cry out by day, but you do not answer, / by night, and am not silent" (Ps. 22:1-2).

Pray that this does not happen to you.

Session 5. Swords into plowshares for the nations

Micah 4:1-13

Chapter 3 ended with one of the harshest oracles of the whole Old Testament: Jerusalem, the symbol of hope and confidence, will become a heap of rubble. God's judgment of the people will be shocking. What does this tell us about God's purpose for the people of God? Will this be the end of Israel? Has God given up on them?

No. That's Micah's firm response. With startling suddenness, the mood changes in chapter 4. The first oracle, verses 1-5, is one of the best known passages from the Prophets. It is one of the most hopeful texts of the whole Old Testament. In this vision of the future, peace rather than war reigns supreme. Salvation and redemption then continue to be the message in the remainder of the chapter. What a contrast to 3:12!

All nations turn toward the chief mountain: 4:1-5
1. Read these first five verses slowly. They express a powerful and eternal hope. Which line (or lines) impresses you most?

Why does this line appeal so strongly to you?

---

2. In the NIV, the oracle begins with the words "In the last days." Other versions speak of the "latter days." This second translation is probably the better one.

When we hear the words *last days*, our thoughts likely move to the final ending of all history, that time when Christ will return, and history, as we know it, will end. But this is not what is implied by the words used by Micah. Rather, these are the words used by the prophets when they began to speak of a future designed by God. In that future time, the troubles of the present will be overcome. God will deal directly with the events of this world with power and purpose. All creation will prosper. When this happens, it does not mean that the end of the world has come. It only means that God is acting in new and decisive ways. In the verses that follow, Micah shares a vision of those days he is looking forward to.

3. The focus of verse 1 is on the "mountain of the LORD'S temple." Notice how this was also the object of the last line of 3:12. But now the message is different, very different. We read that it will become "chief among the mountains," and that "it will be raised above the hills." What do you suppose this may mean?

_____

_____

_____

_____

4. Verses 2-5 can be seen as giving the meaning of verse 1. We will study them in some detail since they contain so much content.

Earlier, 1:2 called on all peoples to pay attention. And yet the oracles that followed dealt only with Israel because God's actions with Israel were to be a sign to the nations that God wants justice. God expected justice in Israel, and God expects it from all other groups of people. When the nations realize this, they themselves become part of the action. They are drawn to the mountain of God. There they face God.

Verses 2-3 report at least two things God will do when this takes place (both are described in more than one way). Describe them in your own words.

a) _____

_____

b) _____

_____

What will be the results of these actions?

a) _____

_____

b) _____

_____

Fearless under the shade of the fig tree

5. Verse 4 speaks of the absence of fear. In Micah's world, nothing produced as much fear in the hearts of the people as the threat of war. First came starvation (as the result of the blockade of a city) and then death. In the latter days, when God brings peace, that fear will be gone.

What do you see as the major causes of fear today?

_____

_____

_____

_____

Verses 2 and 3 suggest that God's teaching (or law—they are really the same) and judgment will produce a peace that will put an end to all such fears.

The way Micah speaks of such a time without fear is most striking—"every man will sit under his own vine/ and under his own fig tree." This was the dream of an

Israelite farmer. He would be able to farm his land in peace, undisturbed by anyone.

What symbols or pictures could you use to describe a setting free of the fears you mentioned above?

_____

_____

_____

6. Verse 5 opens by admitting that in the present time (that is, before the latter days), the people of the nations worship their own gods. This is not a statement of the way things should be: just a reflection of what Israel saw happening in the world around it. Over against this, faithful Israel makes its commitment: it will follow forever the God who led them through the Exodus.

7. The vision of a world without war is one shared by almost all people of all times. It is striking that this is one of the few passages in the Bible found at more than one place. Read it in Isaiah 2:1-5. What is the major difference between these two passages?

_____

_____

How do you think it might have happened that this passage is attributed to both Micah and Isaiah?

_____

_____

_____

We're living in the latter days

8. Applying this passage to our time is not simple. On the one hand, it is clear that it still has not been fully fulfilled. List a few signs from life today which make this clear.

_____

_____

_____

_____

On the other hand, it is not enough to see this passage as simply speaking of the future with no message for us today. And yet this is how these passages concerning latter days are sometimes interpreted. Such an approach is not good enough, and needs to be rejected. There are at least two reasons for saying this.

First of all, the passage was found to be meaningful in Old Testament times. Israel saw God's word to it in this oracle. The fact that it was included in two books of the Bible confirms this point. Since it was seen as a relevant word from God to a people 2500 years ago, we surely shouldn't see it as merely dealing with the future.

Secondly, we live after the time of Christ. The New Testament speaks of the kingdom of God both as having arrived with Christ's coming, and as an experience yet to come.

Compare the latter days of the prophets to the kingdom of God of the New Testament. The latter days are a future time which only God can bring about. But they are also part of a present experience for those who recognize God's control in their lives. The church is called to live in the reality of the latter days—the kingdom of God.

What can this passage then say to us? Let me point to two possibilities.

a) This passage makes it clear that the reconciliation God seeks is for all people, not just Israel. In a sense, this is an Old Testament prelude to the commission of Acts 1:8. Record this verse here.

_____

_____

_____

In the New Testament, the spreading of the gospel to the Gentiles is not in conflict with the vision of the prophets of the Old Testament. Rather, it is a fulfillment of it. According to Acts 1:8, we, as God's witnesses, should be deeply involved in the work of reaching out to others.

How is the church (as "the mountain of the LORD's temple") drawing people to God as these verses suggest it should? What could the church do to improve on this mission?

_____

_____

_____

b) The peace of verses 3 and 4 follows verse 2 which pictures God teaching and the people obeying. Chapter 3 made it clear that justice comes from obedience. In other words, the church will draw people to God as its obedience to God brings peace.

In what things that your congregation is doing do you see peace being produced?

_____

_____

What more could your congregation do?

_____

_____

Verse 4 speaks of training for war. What can we do to train for peace?

_____

_____

_____

_____

Values of the world turned upside down: 4:6-13
1. These verses assume that the punishment announced in chapters 1-3 is near, or has already come. God's overarching purpose of salvation will overcome. The phrase "in that day" is similar in meaning to "in the last days" of 4:1.
   Who is the object of God's action in verse 6?

_____

_____

   In the Old Testament, the term _remnant_ (v. 7) may imply something hopeful (not all will be destroyed—a remnant will survive) or something bad (only a few will make it through the punishment). What does _remnant_ suggest here?

_____

   Today, we often think strength means independence, and the ability to make one's own decisions. Here in verse 7, however, the opposite is true. God will make the lame and weak strong by ruling over them. Strength is not in conflict with God's rule, but a product of it.
   List some other ways in which God's rule turns the values of the world upside down.

_____

_____

_____

   2. Verses 8-10 seem to reflect the agony of a city under siege, with an enemy army camped outside its walls. The

king is either absent or powerless. It seems sure that the people in the city will soon be captured and dragged off to a foreign country. The present suffering is compared to the pains of a woman in labor. But God is not absent or powerless. God will redeem the people from their exile. The punishment was deserved, but it is not final.

3. Compare verses 11-12 to Psalm 2:1-6. Write down some of the ideas that these two passages have in common.

_____

_____

_____

4. In this passage (6-13), which verses imply that God is in control?

_____

_____

_____

_____

How would you describe God's control of events in our time? List some examples.

_____

_____

_____

_____

_____

_____

No training for war anymore

I get excited when I read the first oracle of this chapter. A time is coming when "peoples will stream" to God for instruction, and when peace will reign supreme. What a time that will be! It is hard to imagine such a world in a day when the church appears to be on the decline, and when violence dominates the news. And yet this is the vision Micah sets before us. Here is hope that things will change.

The pull and tug between things as they are now and the hope for the future is not new to us today. Micah felt this in his time as he shows us in verse 5. Although other peoples were still following their own gods, Israel promised to walk in the name of the true God forever. Here, Israel committed itself to the ways and word of God in the present, in the time before this vision became a universal fact. This is also the claim of the church.

If this is so, however, then this vision of hope needs to determine what we do now. This means we will be witnesses for the God who will convert weapons of war into implements of peace and production.

We can only do this if we clearly reject all weapons and ways which take away peace. These do not defend us, but rather are signs that today many people still walk in the ways of their gods. When we count on such weapons to protect us we have given ourselves to their gods, and thus we cannot be witnesses for the true God. May this vision give us the courage to start walking after the Prince of Peace today.

Session 6. Cut by the shepherd of peace

Micah 5:1-15

Salvation is the central theme of the Bible, both in the Old Testament and in the New Testament. Genesis 1—2 describes God as Creator of all, and the human as the high point of creation.

But these chapters also make it clear that although man and woman have been created in the image of God, they tend naturally to use their freedom to rebel. They sin against God. Genesis 12 then describes the call of Abraham and Sarah for the purpose of bringing blessing to all peoples. This theme reaches a climax in Jesus Christ, but it is also at the center of the rest of the Bible.

This theme of salvation is present even in the prophets, despite the fact that they often proclaim punishment. But the purpose of the punishment is to turn people back to God. Yet, in the prophetic books, punishment is never God's last word.

Whereas Micah 1—3 stressed the theme of punishment, chapters 4—5 now declare that God's plan of salvation will not be frustrated. In chapter 5, the text for this session, this salvation includes deliverance and cleansing.

One came out of Bethlehem: 5:1-4
1. The NIV prints each verse of this well-known passage as a separate unit. This is proper, since each verse deals with a different idea. Take note of this as you write down the main point of each verse.

5:1 _____

_____

_____

5:2 _____

_____

_____

5:3 _____

_____

_____

5:4 _____

_____

_____

2. Verse 1 gives the setting for this oracle. What kind of situation does this verse assume?

_____

_____

_____

3. 1 Samuel 16:1-13 describes how Samuel anoints David to become king of Israel. This gives the background to this oracle of Micah, especially to verse 2. The reference to Bethlehem at once reminded Micah's listeners or readers of David who came from Bethlehem, about 300 years before the time of Micah. The last two lines of this verse point the people back to that time. Read 1 Samuel 16:1-13.

In this passage, *anoint* and *choose* really have the same meaning. The anointing of someone for a task was a sign that God has chosen that person for the task. How many times is some form of either of these two terms used in 1 Samuel 16:1-13?

anoint _____

choose _____

Why do you think they are used so often?

_____

_____

Although neither of these terms is used in Micah 5:2, the fact that this ruler "will come for me" brings out the same point.

Linking David and Messiah and Christ

4. Micah 5:2 is one of a number of Old Testament passages which is quoted in the New Testament as pointing to the birth of Jesus. When the Magi (or wise men) asked King Herod where the Christ was to be born, his counselors quoted this verse (Matt. 2:1-6). Why, do you think, did they do this?

_____

_____

Let me try to explain the logic of the link between David and the Christ.

David was surely the most important king in Israel's history. During his reign, Israel became a powerful nation. This was Israel's golden age. In 2 Samuel 7:16, God announced to David that his throne would be established forever.

When, later, Israel experienced crisis, and even exile, it held to its faith in this promise. It longed for a new David, a leader who would deliver them from their enemies. A number of the Old Testament prophets proclaimed such a message. They announced that God would send a deliverer to the people.

Since David (like other kings) was anointed for his task, and since the Hebrew term for "anointed" is *Messiah*, this tradition is called messianic expectation. *Christ* is the Greek form of Messiah. Micah 5:2 is part of this tradition. Thus when the Magi ask where the Christ (Messiah, or anointed one) is to be born, Micah 5:2 is read.

How do you think the Israelite people of Micah's day would have understood this verse? Remember the setting given to this oracle in verse 1.

_____

_____

_____

_____

How was Jesus different from this Messiah who was expected?

_____

_____

Despite these differences, it is the claim of the New Testament, and the faith of the church, that Jesus is the fulfillment of this passage. What does this suggest about the way one should understand prophecy?

_____

_____

_____

5. According to the second line of verse 2, Bethlehem will produce this ruler even though it is "small among the clans of Judah." Compare this with 1 Samuel 16:1-13. Why is Jesse surprised that David is the one chosen to be king?

_____

_____

Why do you think David may have been chosen rather than one of his older brothers?

_____

This theme is also reflected in other accounts where someone is called to an important position. Notice this in the following passages. Record the name of the person called.

Judges 6:14-15 _____

1 Samuel 9:21 _____

What does this tell us about the way God chooses people?

_____

_____

_____

How could we follow this example when we elect / appoint / choose people for tasks in the church?

_____

_____

_____

6. Verse 3 tries, it seems, to explain the delay in the coming of this ruler. Israel waited many years before this event took place. The statement "when she who is in labor gives birth" is probably not meant to imply that this will happen shortly, that is, within the next nine months, but is a reference back to 4:9-10. It thus describes the nature of the time before the ruler comes—it is a time of pain and suffering, like the experiences of a woman in labor.

7. The shepherd imagery is again used in verse 4 (remember 2:12 in Session 3). Jesus speaks of himself as the good shepherd in John 10:11-18. What trait of the good shepherd is mentioned three times in these verses?

_____

_____

How can this trait be brought together with the verses in Micah which also speak of the expected one as a ruler?

_____

_____

_____

The dew of Jacob and the lion: 5:5-9

1. Here are two more oracles proclaiming God's action for the people. The first one speaks of Assyria trying to invade, but being unsuccessful. This is a reversal of history. So often Israel had experienced the horrors of a successful invasion by an enemy. The term _Assyria_ in this passage may be symbolic of any enemy force. The "he" of verse 6 is, probably a reference back to the ruler / shepherd / messiah of verses 1-4.

2. Verses 7 and 8 compare the remnant of Jacob to dew and a lion. Dew plays an important role in Palestine during the rainless months. It supplies just enough moisture so that vineyards can remain quite healthy despite the absence of rain. Dew seems to come out of nowhere, is hardly noticed, and yet can be extremely effective. How is this a helpful symbol for the remnant of Jacob?

_____

_____

_____

_____

The lion is a symbol of strength and superiority. How would you relate this symbol to the dew?

_____

_____

Do you think it is fair to apply this oracle to the church of today? What would its message mean for the church?

_____

_____

_____

_____

Cutting out the things that poison: 5:10-15
1. Notice the phrase used to date this oracle: "in that day." The last place this phrase was used was in 4:6, at the beginning of the announcement that God would take the lame / remnant and make of them a strong nation. That was clearly an oracle of salvation. This one is less clear, but the presence of the same opening phrase suggests that it speaks of the same time, and thus should probably be interpreted in line with 4:6-7. Let's see what this might mean.
2. Write down the verb (or, action word) that is most prominent in this passage.

_____

If you have another Bible translation, see what word is used there.

_____

The NIV is not as helpful as it might be in the translation offered here. The Hebrew term used is a form of the simple verb "to cut." This verb is used at other points for the removal of people from Israel who have transgressed God's law. The emphasis is on the taking away of the object, rather than on the destruction of the object. This passage thus speaks of the *purification*, or cleansing of the people of all those things that poison their relationship to God.

3. List all those items that are to be eliminated, or cut out of God's people. Separate those in verses 10-11 from those in verses 12-14.

Verses 10-11 _____

_____

Verses 12-14 _____

_____

What do the items in verses 12-14 have in common? (Note the footnote in the NIV about Asherah poles.)

_____

_____

_____

_____

The common feature of the items listed in verses 10-11 is a little more difficult to discover. Read Isaiah 31:1 for a hint. The strongholds of verse 11 are probably military forts. How would you now describe what God will eliminate according to these two verses?

_____

_____

_____

What are some things you think God might like to cut out of the life of God's people today?

_____

_____

_____

What would God cut out of your life?

_____

_____

4. The final verse of this chapter returns to the theme of the nations. This is the fourth major reference to them, the others being 1:2, 4:1-4, and 5:7-8. What happens to the nations in each of these passages?

1:2 _____

_____

4:1-4 _____

_____

5:7-8 _____

_____

5:15 _____

_____

God's vengeance is seen by Micah as the necessary response of the God of all history to peoples who have witnessed God's actions and who have observed God's rule, but have not submitted to it. Judgment is part of the real world. But as was the case in the judgment of Israel, its purpose is not revenge but repentance and cleansing.

Salvation and the pain that purifies

While I found the vision of 4:1-5 exciting, I find the oracle of 5:10-15 sobering. Here Micah clearly states that God will destroy, or cut out, various parts of Israelite life, and this in a chapter devoted to the good news of deliverance. This I find disturbing for two reasons.

First of all, this passage reminds me that deliverance, although good news, may also include purging or cleansing, and this may be painful. Deliverance means salvation, but it also means leaving behind a life to which one has grown accustomed.

Salvation may thus bring pain. Israel's Exodus from Egypt was by no means easy. In fact, at a number of points, the people longed for the "security" of slavery in Egypt. This is so true to life. Both individuals and the church may experience that the road of salvation may include cleansing events.

Secondly, this passage forces me to ask myself where I improperly put my reliance. Micah suggests that Israel placed its trust in military equipment and religious rituals. Today we can count on our social status, on our economic security, on our role in the church, or on our religious knowledge to deliver us. But none of these can really carry us through. These are all the "work of your hands" of verse 13.

When God purifies, these are what may be cut away. May God give me the courage to stop relying on the works of my hands, and put my complete trust in God.

Session 7. Mountains and hills hear God's complaint

Micah 6:1-16

To some extent, Micah 1—5 was a complete section. It began and ended with a reference to all peoples or nations, and it included both announcements of judgment and salvation.

Micah 6 is now a new section, with a special and formal structure. In Old Testament studies, this is often called a "covenant lawsuit." Let me explain.

At the heart of the Old Testament is the affirmation that God made a covenant with Israel. This covenant was confirmed (or "signed") at Mount Sinai following the Exodus from Egypt. Exodus 24 describes the formal covenant-making ceremony. In this ritual, the Law is read to the people, and they seal the covenant by saying, "We will do everything the LORD has said; we will obey."

A covenant lawsuit is then a formal charge against Israel saying that it has broken the covenant, and not kept its side of the agreement. One could easily compare it to the proceedings of a court trial. God is the plaintiff, or the accuser; Israel is the defendant, or the accused. Let us now look at the chapter.

Lodging a charge against Israel: 6:1-16
1. List all the terms in verses 1-2 which point to the legal form of this oracle.

Notice before whom the case is to be heard. Write down those parts of nature mentioned.

_____

_____

These parts of nature serve as witnesses in the trial. This, no doubt, sounds rather unusual to us, but it can be explained. Israel understood its covenant with God along the lines of the political treaties of its time. When two nations made a treaty, they would use their gods as witnesses. The forces of nature were often also listed, whether also as gods or simply as powerful forces is not clear.

Israel recognized only one God, so, naturally, the people could not use gods as their witnesses. Parts of nature, however, are mentioned at a number of points in the Old Testament as witnesses (for example, Deut. 30:19; Isa. 1:2). Since these elements of nature are spoken of when referring to the making of the covenant with God, they are also called upon when Israel is accused of breaking the covenant.

2. Record the language and images used of God's relationship to Israel in the following passages:

Isaiah 1:2 _____

Deuteronomy 32:19 _____

Jeremiah 2:13 _____

Hosea 11:1 _____

Hosea 2:2 _____
What general impression do these phrases give?

_____

_____

_____

What phrase, or picture, do you find helpful for describing God's present relationship to God's people?

_____

_____

_____

Remember the righteous acts

Verses 3 and 5 open with the touching words: "My people." This is one of the most important phrases describing God's bond to Israel. God had chosen Israel as God's special possession. God had redeemed this people from the slavery of Egypt. And now they have rejected God's ways. Like a hurt parent, God questions Israel—"What have I done to you?" It appears as if Israel has accused God of not being faithful. Israel is challenged to give evidence. But there is no response.

3. God continues presenting the case against Israel by countering the complaints implied by verse 3. The great salvation events of Israel's history are noted—the Exodus, the wilderness wanderings, and the gift of the Promised Land.

Identify the following names, and tell why they are used in this passage. The scriptural references given should help.

Egypt _____

_____ (6:4)

Moses _____

_____ (6:4; Exod. 3:10)

Aaron _____

_____ (Exod. 4:14-17)

Miriam _____

_____ (Exod. 15:20-21)

Balak, king of Moab _____

_____

_____

_____ (Num. 22:1-10)

Baalam, son of Beor _____

_____

_____

_____ (Num. 23:1-12)

Shittim and Gilgal were campsites of Israel as the people entered the Promised Land.

4. Read Exodus 3:7-10. This is part of the call of Moses. Here God announces to Moses what God will do. How would you describe such a God?

_____

_____

_____

_____

A number of passages in the Old Testament describe God by telling what God has done for Israel. Read the following, and pick out the events which appear to be the most important.

Exodus 20:2 _____

_____

Deuteronomy 6:20-25 _____

_____

Deuteronomy 26:5-10 _____

_____

Joshua 24:2-13 _____

Israel is often told to remember these key events, and God's role in them (v. 5). (See, for example, Deut. 5:15; 15:15.) Think of some important events in your life in which God was at work.

_____

_____

_____

In what events in the life or history of your church or denomination has God acted?

_____

_____

_____

The prophets of the Old Testament take it for granted that remembering the events in which God acted will encourage obedience to the God of those events. What might you do to have a better memory?

_____

_____

_____

What could your church/denomination do?

_____

_____

Christmas and Easter are festivals which recall key New Testament salvation events. Do you think these re-membrances promote obedience? How could our celebration of them be improved so that they might promote better remembrance and better obedience?

_____

_____

_____

_____

5. Back to the court case: finally, the defendant (the people) respond: "What should we have done?" or "What should we do?" What are the people who ask the four questions in verses 6-7 thinking about? What type of action do they expect will be required?

_____

_____

_____

_____

Notice the rising cost in what is offered. The final question volunteers child sacrifice which goes beyond what Israelite religion allowed. The prophets condemned it, and Israel's tradition called for a substitution for human sacrifice. The story of Abraham and Isaac in Genesis 22 reflects this. And yet it is suggested. In the religions of that time, this would have been an action indicating total devotion and obedience. So, in a desperate attempt at defense, even this extreme sacrifice is offered.

The answer of verse 8 rejects all the questions of verses 6-7. God does not require sacrifice or gifts: God requires a special way of life. Here is one of the most important statements of the Bible. This is the heart of the message preached by the prophets.

Compare verses 6-8 with the words of a few other prophets. Write down the terms, or specific acts called for.

1 Samuel 15:22-23 _____

_____

Isaiah 1:10-17 _____

_____

_____

_____

Jeremiah 6:19-20 _____

_____

Amos 5:21-24 _____

_____

The rejection and denial of sacrifices and ritual reflected in these verses do not imply that sacrifice and
worship are wrong. The prophet meant that no sacrifice or
act of worship can substitute for obedience.

It seems that the natural tendency in religion is to rely
on the formal part of religion for one's security. We do not
have a sacrificial system anymore, but this temptation to
trust in ritual is as much present now as in the days of
Micah.

What things in our Christian practice might modern-
day prophets attack?

_____

_____

_____

_____

Three good deeds worth doing

The three key terms of verse 8 can use some explanation.
To *act justly*, or to do justice, is not merely following some
specific rules, or obeying the law of the land. Rather, this
deed speaks to a whole way of life. It implies living one's

life in such a way that God's will is promoted everywhere.

The nature of God's justice is reflected most clearly in God's actions in the Exodus. Here God entered into the affairs of humans in order to redeem a group of slaves from the hands of the Egyptians. They were unable to help themselves, so God helped them. To act justly is a way of living which reflects this kind of concern for all people.

The Hebrew term here translated *to love mercy* is hard to define since it is used in so many different ways. Other common translations of this term include "loving kindness" or "covenant faithfulness." In this verse, it serves to make clear the meaning of the first term.

Loving mercy includes the idea of being faithful to the requirements or expectations of a relationship. But remember how Jesus described what it means to respond in the right way to one's neighbor: he told the story of the Good Samaritan (Luke 10:29-37). All humans are brothers and sisters and neighbors. To love mercy means to be faithful and merciful in all these relationships.

Whereas the first two terms are common biblical terms for what God requires, *to walk humbly with your God* is unique to this passage. It has been defined as "attending the will and way of God." This involves action, and thus is more than simply doing your own thing without attracting attention. God's actions in the history of Israel give content to each of these terms. Israel was expected to act like that in response.

Think of a few actions you have observed recently which could serve as examples of these terms.

Act justly:

_____

_____

_____

_____

Love mercy:

_____

_____

_____

_____

Walk humbly with God:

_____

_____

_____

_____

Dishonest scales and false weights

6. The covenant lawsuit concludes with two further charges (vv. 10-12 and v. 16a) and two announcements of punishment (vv. 13-15 and v. 16b). Whereas the accusation of chapters 1—3 tended to focus on the leaders, here all who have the chance to cheat their neighbors are included. These verses give examples of ignoring the requirements of verse 8.

Why do you think so many of these verses deal with the use of money and material possessions?

_____

_____

_____

_____

Omri and Ahab were two kings of Israel (the Northern Kingdom) who were noted for their sins against God. Read 1 Kings 16:25-26 and 1 Kings 16:29-33 for ratings of these two kings. What acts of theirs are singled out?

Omri _____

_____

Ahab _____

_____

7. The trial is over. You be the judge. What is your verdict? guilty or not guilty?

_____

What would be your sentence?_____

_____

_____

Accused by Micah on decisions made

Verse 8 is at the center of this chapter. As a result, we spent most of our time in this session examining it and the verses leading up to it. The accusation of verses 10-12 is relevant for our time, however, and deserves some further comments. The impression I receive in these verses is that the moral climate in Israel had fallen to the point where cheating in the marketplace had become so commonplace and accepted by many in the community. After all, "Everyone is doing it."

Micah lashes out at such acts, but in the process hits us as well. Profit is not a dirty word, but when financial gain becomes the controlling force behind one's choices, then sin is present. This is true whether one is in business or not. And this is true whether the actions taken are legal or not.

Many of us stand accused by Micah on this score: Do I declare all my purchases when I pass through customs? Do I keep on asking myself how I can use my friendships for my benefit? Do I ask for cash so I do not need to report it at income tax time? Do I only give when I will receive an income tax deductible receipt? Do I look at a job largely from the standpoint of salary, and what I will receive from it? To act justly (v. 8) means to make the well-being of others our standard rather than only personal gain. May God guide us along this path.

Session 8. No other God like our God

Micah 7:1-20

Today we want to study the last chapter of Micah. In some ways, this chapter is different from the rest of the book. It is more like a psalm than a passage from a prophetic book. This is true both of its style and its content. Like the psalms, it could very well have been used or recited as part of public worship. And like many of the psalms, it moves from lament to praise. We will observe some of these likenesses in this study.

Even though the chapter is somewhat different from the book, it still is a proper ending to the book. It contains many of the themes covered in the book, and so can serve as a review of Micah. We will also take note of these themes.

It is sometimes asked whether chapter 7 comes from a time later than Micah. Verse 11, for example, speaks of building walls, a statement which would make more sense later in Israel's history when the walls of Jerusalem had been destroyed. The evidence is not final, however. And even should it come from a later time, it is now very much part of Micah—it has been integrated with the book. It is thus fitting that we conclude the study of Micah with it.

Praying during dark and evil days: Psalms 12 and 14
1. Two psalms which are somewhat similar to Micah 7 are Psalms 12 and 14 (also the same as Psalm 53). Turn to

them in your Bible, and answer the following questions:

What is the mood of the psalmist?

Psalm 12 _____

_____

Psalm 14 _____

_____

Why does the psalmist feel this way?

Psalm 12 _____

_____

_____

Psalm 14 _____

_____

_____

What does the psalmist say about God?

Psalm 12 _____

_____

_____

Psalm 14 _____

_____

_____

Can you detect a change of mood in the psalm as it moves to its conclusion? How would you describe this change?

Psalm 12 _____

_____

_____

Psalm 14 _____

_____

_____

Have you ever felt like either of these two psalmists? If so, what caused you to feel that way?

_____

_____

_____

_____

What did you do about it?

_____

_____

_____

_____

Psalms 12 and 14 are two examples of psalms of lament, or psalms of petition. This is the most common type of psalm, a prayer to God from people who are in despair, or people who do not feel God's presence. Some reflect deep depression. And yet, amazingly, almost all contain some expression of confidence in God, or conclude on a note of praise.

No summer fruit for the gleaner

2. Now read all of Micah 7. List the likenesses between it and Psalms 12 and 14. Take note both of content and style or mood.

_____

_____

_____

_____

_____

3. Micah 7 may once have been a psalm of lament used in Israelite worship, but it is also very much part of Micah. It can be seen as a response to the announcement of judgment in chapter 6. It is not clear who the speaker is meant to be. Could it be Micah? Or is it some righteous person in Jerusalem? Or is it, as some have suggested, meant to be understood as coming from the city of Jerusalem itself. Notice that the accusation of 6:9 was addressed to the city. Which answer would you choose?

_____

Why did you choose this answer?

_____

_____

Lovers of mercy swept away
4. The lament itself is largely found in verses 1-6. Verse 1 gives a general introduction. Verses 2-4 tend to focus on public life, and verses 5-6 on the home.

The term translated "godly" in verse 2 of the NIV comes from the same Hebrew word translated "to love mercy" in 6:8. In other words, this verse shows that what is asked for in 6:8 is absent from the land.

What type of activity do you think verse 2b refers to?

_____

_____

What other passages in Micah do verses 3-4 remind you of? List a few.

_____

_____

_____

Verse 5 moves from neighbor to friend to wife. Verse 6 continues to focus on the person's home. One cannot even trust the family unit. This would have been even more alarming in that society in which the stability and harmony of the family was of such great importance. The extended family was then the basic unit for almost all of life. Today we have many organizations or clubs which provide some of the needs which the family served in that time.

5. The first half of the chapter reaches its high point in verse 7. Despite the turmoil and chaos reflected by the writer in verses 1-6, the prophet still has confidence in God. Write down the two verbs used to describe what the speaker will do.

_____   _____

These two terms are not action oriented. The response of the speaker is not what we might normally expect. We live in a time and on a continent where action reigns supreme. "What are you going to *do* about it?" is the common question. But sometimes nothing can be done, and then the only faithful response is to wait upon God. One scholar has said:

> In a present full of violence and betrayal the speaker turns to a future in which he can hope . . . He does not give up and surrender to depression, but "waits," the most powerful form of action by the helpless who express in their waiting the knowledge that God comes to them in the form of salvation.

Standing tall in time of trouble
6. Review 3:5-8. Compare these verses with 7:1-7. What phrase do both 3:8 and 7:7 begin with?

_____

How are these two verses (3:8 and 7:7) tied to the verses before them?

_____

_____

_____

How do you think the confidence expressed in these two verses was gained?

_____

_____

_____

7. Micah 7:1-7 seems to hint that the speaker is alone in his concern. All other faithful friends have disappeared— even this person's spouse cannot be trusted. This is aloneness at its worst. Such feelings sometimes come. A number of the psalms express similar thoughts. Elijah, a prophet of Israel some 100 years before Micah, also felt this way.

How does Elijah describe his situation (1 Kings 19:10, 14)?

_____

_____

But God did not accept this reading of the scene. What was God's response to Elijah (1 Kings 19:18)?

_____

_____

This may be a warning to us not to get into such a mood too quickly. Evil is powerful and very present. And yet God is more powerful, and there are many who are faithful.

8. Verse 7 is the turning point in this chapter. The tone has changed, and the remainder of the chapter reflects confidence. Although things look bad now, God will act and redemption will take place.

According to verse 9, Israel is fallen and in darkness. In verse 10, the speaker admits that this is because of sin. Could this chapter reflect the fulfillment of Micah's earlier prophecies?

_____

_____

Verse 9 uses the word *case*. When was the last time this term was used in Micah?

_____

How is it used differently now?

_____

_____

_____

When God's people are guilty, then a trial leads to judgment. But when God's people are faithful, or when punishment has been completed, a trial leads to vindication and a verdict of not guilty.

In the days of God's justice
9. What does this passage (vv. 10-12) say about the future with regard to:

enemies? _____

_____

_____

the city and country? _____

_____

_____

the exiles (v. 12)? _____

_____

Bashan and Gilead are mentioned in verse 14. These two areas of Palestine were famous for fertile land and good crops. This verse thus announces that a time will come when prosperity will again be present.

10. Verse 15 gives the background and basis for the speaker's faith. When was this event last mentioned in Micah?

_____

11. The enemies and other nations are spoken of in verses 10, 13, and 16-17. Such passages always raise problems for the Christian. It has been suggested that such thinking about retribution must disappear in the shadow of the cross. What do you think?

_____

_____

Compare verses 16-17 with 4:1-5. Do you think they could be speaking of the same thing? Note that "to fear the LORD" usually means to honor and obey God. How does each passage help you understand the other?

_____

_____

_____

12. What do verses 18-20 tell us about God?

_____

_____

_____

_____

Notice the use of the three important words in the Old Testament for wrongdoing in verses 18-19. Note that all will be forgiven. What are these words?

Do the descriptions of God reflected in verses 18-19 fit with the preaching of Micah in the rest of the book? At what points are they the same?

At what points in these verses, do you notice something said about God that is different from what is said about God in the rest of Micah?

13. What has surprised you most about the Book of Micah?

Did you discover anything in this book that bothers you?

If so, talk to someone about it. Remember also that it is helpful to see each part of the Bible as part of the rest of

the Bible, and to interpret the difficult passages with help
from the easier.

How would you now sum up the message of Micah?

_____

_____

_____

_____

Final word found in forgiveness
Again I must divide my response to this chapter into two
parts. First of all, I am attracted to verse 7. What does it
mean to *watch* and *hope* in the world of our day? I can't
help but think that this verse must be interpreted in light
of the keynote statement of 6:8. To watch and wait does
not imply that action has no meaning. We are still expected to act justly and love mercy. All of our life still
needs to reflect the justice of God.

The verse does suggest, however, that during some
times and at some places, one needs to recognize that
one's action will not change a bad situation. It seems to
me that this verse thus doesn't excuse inaction, but warns
us not to put too much faith in our efforts. In the end, we
can only trust in the God of our salvation to hear us.

Secondly, I am encouraged by the final three verses of
this chapter. Much of Micah drew attention to the sin of
Israel, and the sure fact of God's punishment. Rebellion
against God and God's way does produce its own rewards.
And yet the final word of this book is not the *no* of punishment but the *yes* of forgiveness. God is a God of love and
caring. This is shown most clearly in the sending of Jesus
Christ to our world.

May each one of us be able to accept this forgiveness,
and live the life of obedience for which this forgiveness
frees us. Amen.